FIVE 5 FINGER PIANO

MY FIRST HYMN BOOK

ISBN 978-1-4234-7403-6

HAL•LEONARD® CORPORATION

7777 W. BLUEMOUND RD. P.O. BOX 13819 MILWAUKEE, WI 53213

In Australia Contact:
Hal Leonard Australia Pty. Ltd.
4 Lentara Court
Cheltenham, Victoria, 3192 Australia
Email: ausadmin@halleonard.com.au

Visit Hal Leonard Online at
www.halleonard.com

Amazing Grace

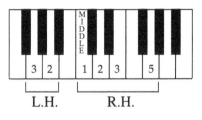

Words by John Newton
Traditional American Melody

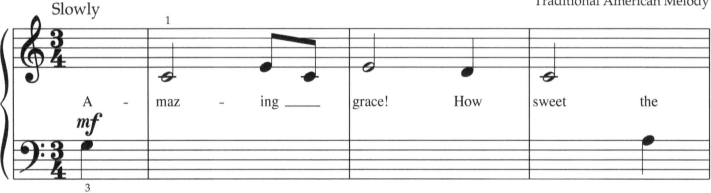

A - maz - ing _____ grace! How sweet the

sound that saved a _____ wretch like

Duet Part (Student plays one octave higher than written.)

Slowly

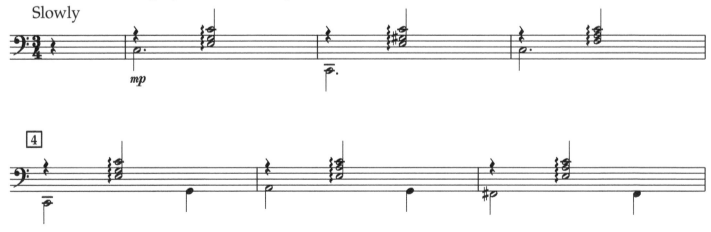

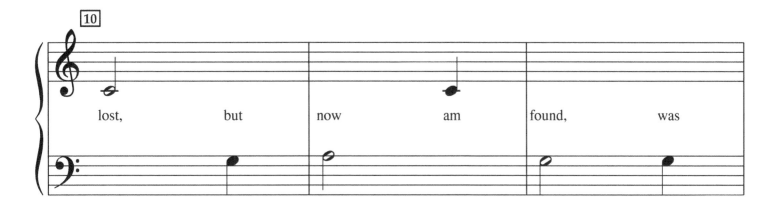

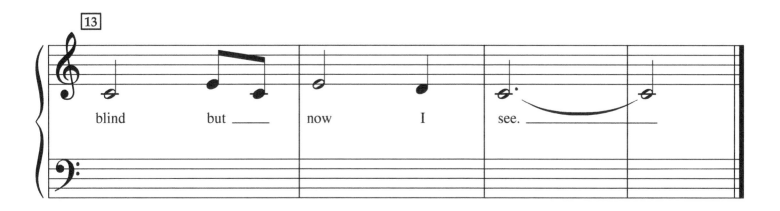

Fairest Lord Jesus

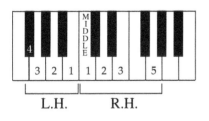

Words from *Münster Gesangbuch*
Music from *Schlesische Volkslieder*

Reverently

Fair - est Lord Je - sus, rul - er of all

mp

na - ture, O Thou of God and ____

Duet Part (Student plays one octave higher than written.)

Reverently

p

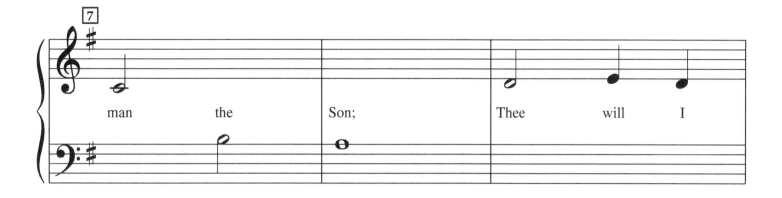

man the Son; Thee will I

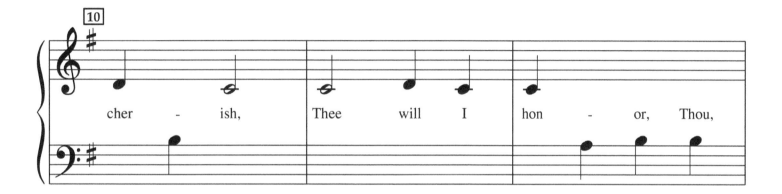

cher - ish, Thee will I hon - or, Thou,

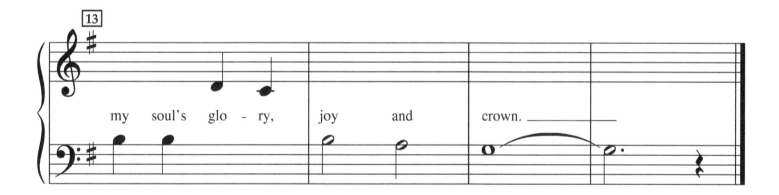

my soul's glo - ry, joy and crown.

I Surrender All

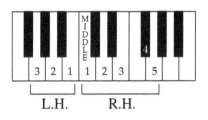

Words by J.W. Van Deventer
Music by W.S. Weeden

Duet Part (Student plays one octave higher than written.)

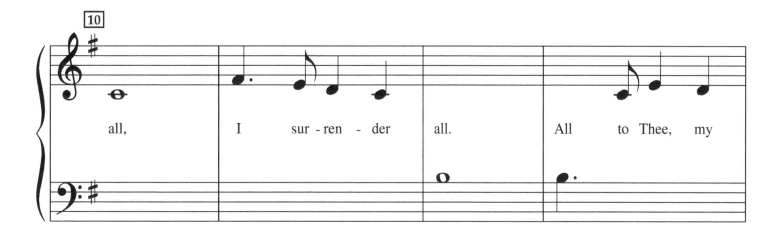

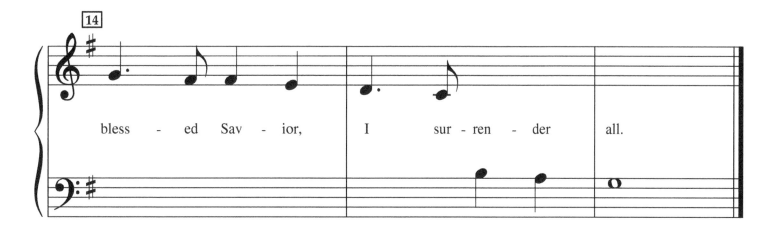

I've Got Peace Like a River

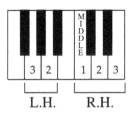

Traditional

Duet Part (Student plays two octaves higher than written.)

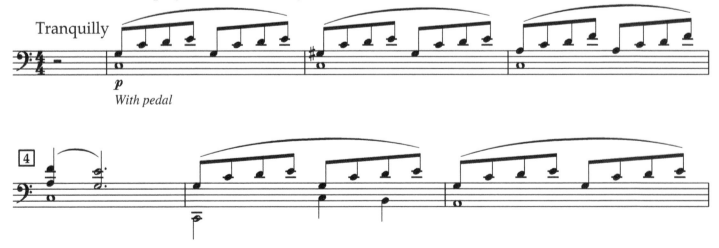

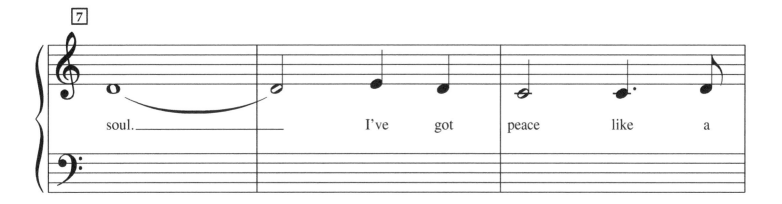

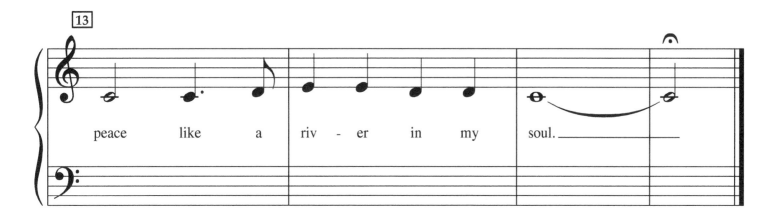

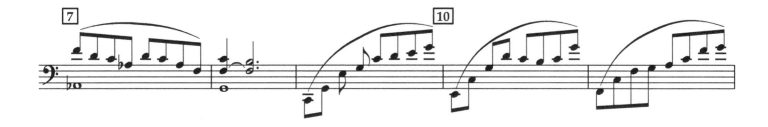

Jesus Loves Even Me
(I Am So Glad)

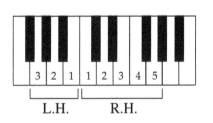

Words and Music by
Philip P. Bliss

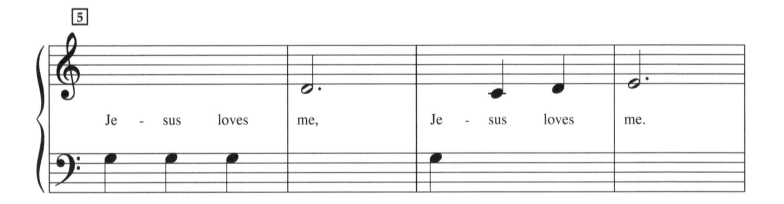

Duet Part (Student plays one octave higher than written.)
Moderately

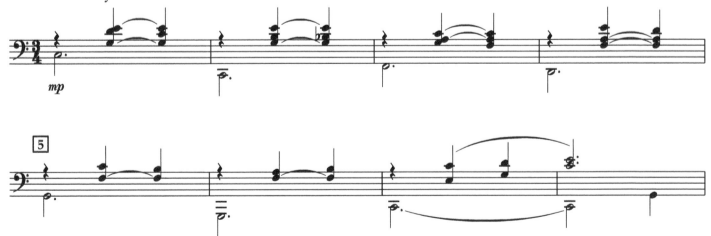

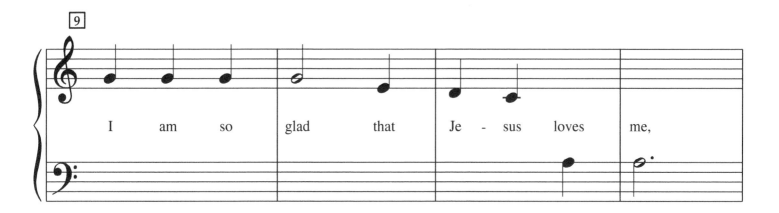

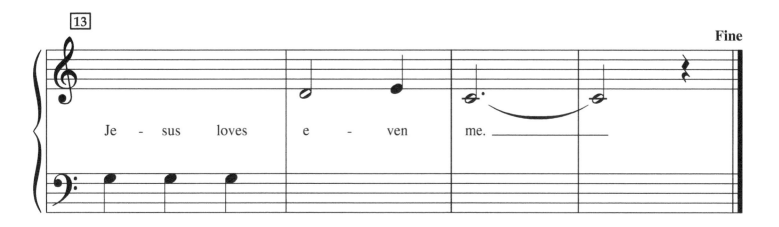

tells   of   His   love   in   the   book   He   has   giv'n.

Won - der - ful   things   in   the   Bi - ble   I   see;

D.C. al Fine

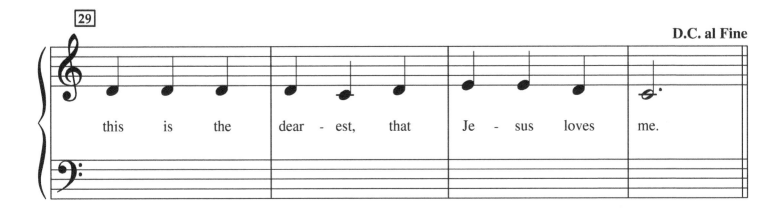

this   is   the   dear - est,   that   Je - sus   loves   me.

D.C. al Fine

God Is So Good

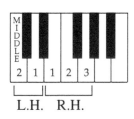

Traditional

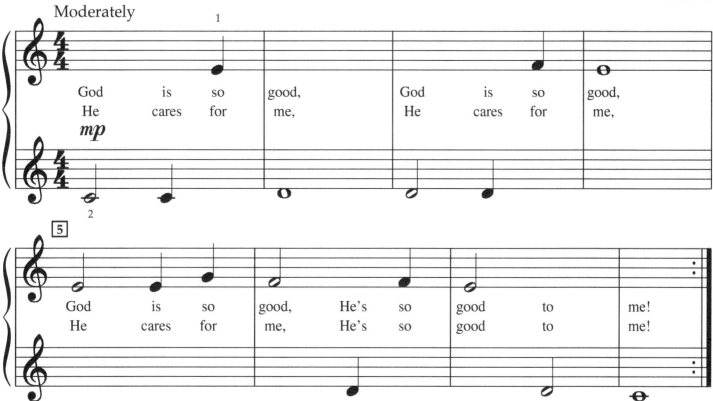

Duet Part (Student plays one octave higher than written.)

Moderately

With pedal

Jesus Loves Me

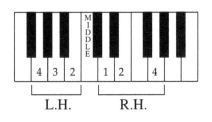

Words by Anna B. Warner
Music by William B. Bradbury

Sweetly

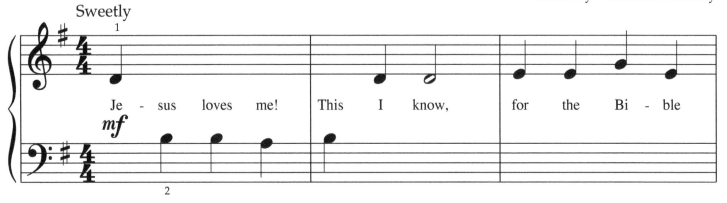

Je - sus loves me! This I know, for the Bi - ble

mf

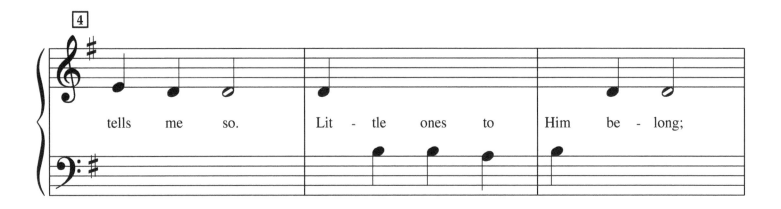

tells me so. Lit - tle ones to Him be - long;

Duet Part

Sweetly

Play 8va throughout

p With pedal

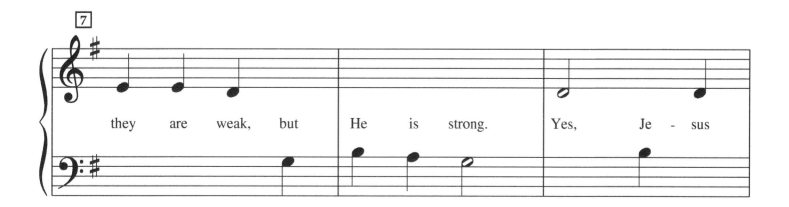

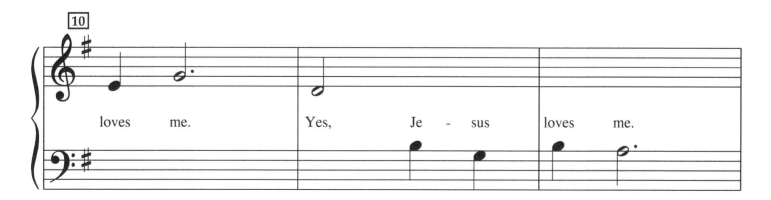

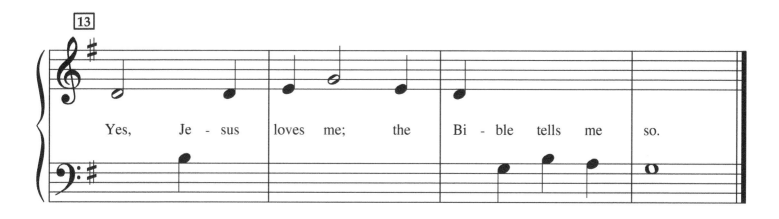

Praise Him, All Ye Little Children

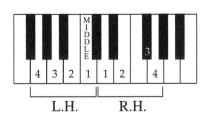

Traditional Words
Music by Carey Bonner

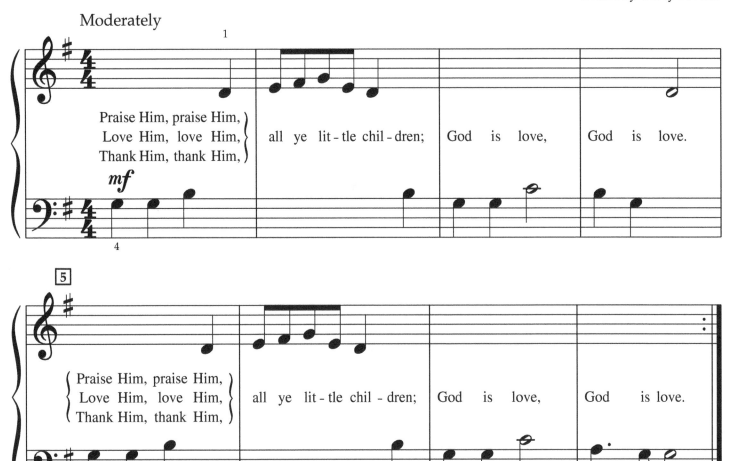

Moderately

Praise Him, praise Him,
Love Him, love Him,
Thank Him, thank Him,
all ye lit-tle chil-dren; God is love, God is love.

Praise Him, praise Him,
Love Him, love Him,
Thank Him, thank Him,
all ye lit-tle chil-dren; God is love, God is love.

Duet Part (Student plays one octave higher than written.)

Moderately

Take My Life and Let It Be

Words by Frances R. Havergal
Music by Henry A. César Malan

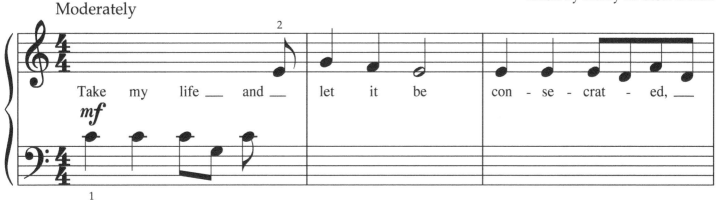

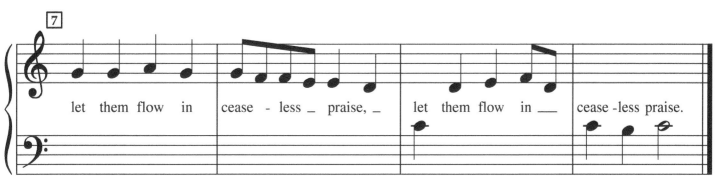

Duet Part (Student plays one octave higher than written.)

Savior, Like a Shepherd Lead Us

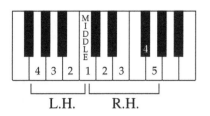

Words from *Hymns for the Young*
Attributed to Dorothy A. Thrupp
Music by William B. Bradbury

Duet Part (Student plays one octave higher than written.)

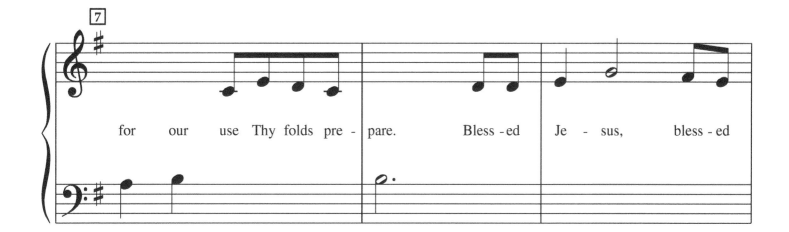

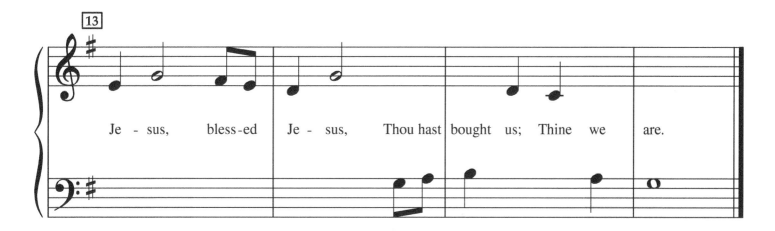

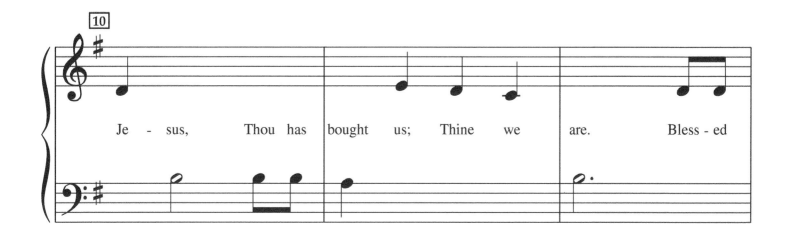

19

'Tis So Sweet to Trust in Jesus

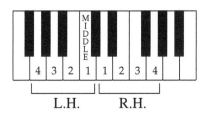

Words by Louisa M.R. Stead
Music by William J. Kirkpatrick

Moderately

'Tis so sweet to trust in Je - sus, Just to take Him at His word, Just to rest up - on His prom - ise,

Duet Part (Student plays one octave higher than written.)

Moderately

mp
With pedal

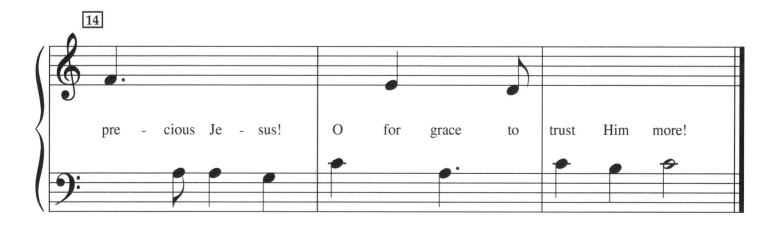

When I Survey the Wondrous Cross

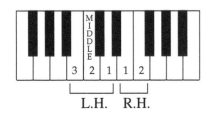

Words by Isaac Watts
Music arranged by Lowell Mason
Based on Plainsong

Slowly

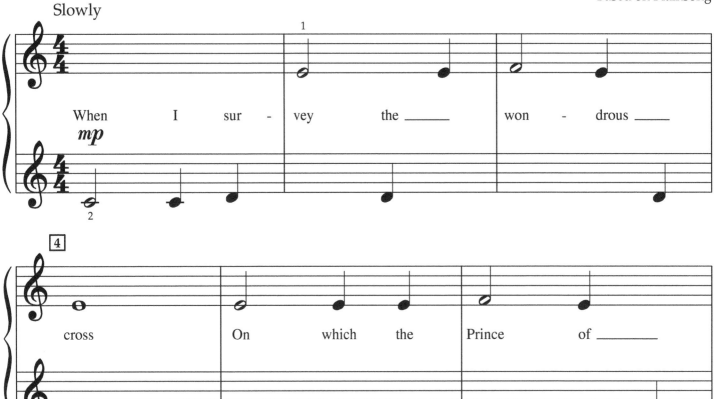

When I sur - vey the _____ won - drous _____ cross On which the Prince of _____

Duet Part (Student plays one octave higher than written.)

Slowly

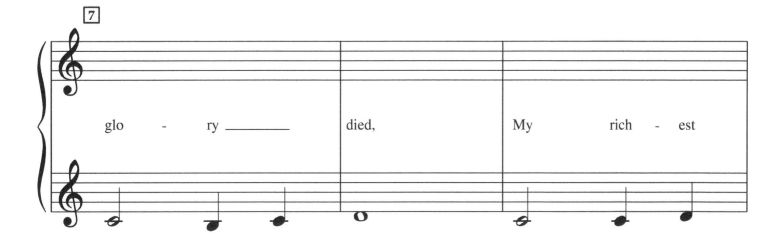

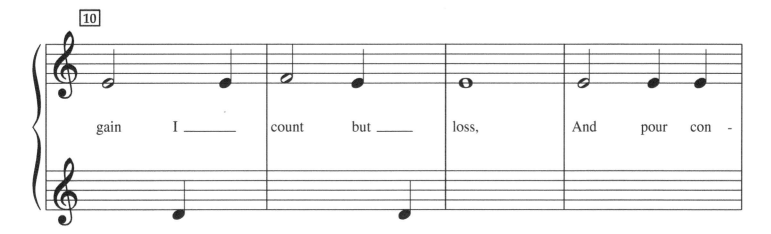

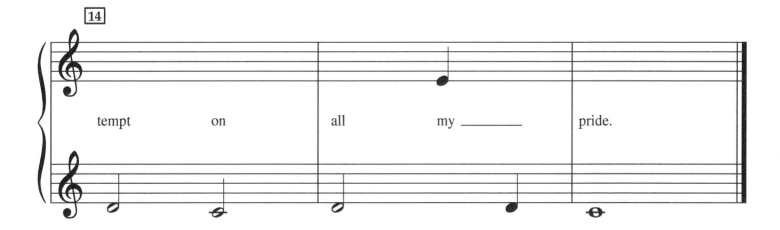

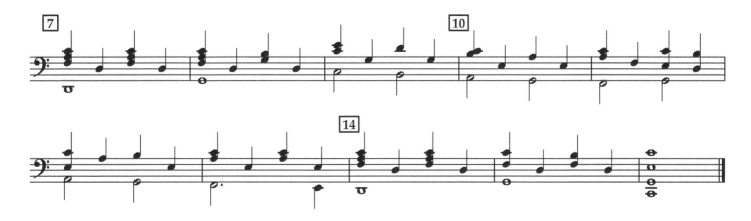

PLAYING PIANO HAS NEVER BEEN EASIER!

Five-Finger Piano songbooks from Hal Leonard are designed for students in their first year of study. They feature single-note melody lines that stay in one position, indicated by a small keyboard diagram at the beginning of each song. Each song also includes lyrics, and beautifully written piano accompaniments that can be played by teachers, parents or more experienced students to give new players a "it sounds so good!" experience.

 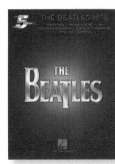   

Adele
00175097   8 songs $9.99

Beatles! Beatles!
00292061   8 songs $8.99

Beatles Favorites
00310369   8 songs $9.99

Beatles Greatest
00310370   7 songs $8.99

The Beatles Hits
00128687   8 songs $8.99

Cartoon Fun
00279151   8 songs $8.99

A Charlie Brown Christmas™
00316069   10 songs $10.99

The Charlie Brown Collection™
00316072   8 songs $8.99

Children's TV Favorites
00311208   8 songs $7.95

Christmas Carols
00236800   10 songs $7.99

Christmas Songs Made Easy
00172307   10 songs $8.99

Christmas Treasures
00290041   8 songs $6.99

Church Songs for Kids
00310613   15 songs $8.99

Classical Favorites
00310611   12 selections....................... $8.99

Classical Themes
00310469   10 songs $7.95

Disney Classics
00311429   7 songs $8.99

Disney Delights
00310195   9 songs $8.99

Disney Favorites
00311038   8 songs $8.99

Disney Latest Movie Hits
00277255   8 songs $10.99

Disney Movie Classics
00123475   8 songs $9.99

Disney Movie Fun
00292067   8 songs $8.99

Disney Songs
00283429   8 songs $9.99

Disney Today
00175218   8 songs $8.99

Disney Tunes
00310375   8 songs $9.99

Disney's Princess Collection
00310847   Volume 1 (7 songs) $10.99
00310848   Volume 2 (7 songs) $14.99

Eensy Weensy Spider & Other Nursery Rhyme Favorites
00310465   11 songs $7.95

First Pop Songs
00123296   8 songs $9.99

Frozen
00130374   7 songs $14.99

Frozen 2
00329705   8 songs $10.99

Fun Songs
00346769   8 songs $8.99

Gershwin Classics
00322126   14 songs $8.95

Hallelujah and Other Songs of Inspiration
00119649   9 songs $7.99

Happy Birthday to You and Other Great Songs
00102097   10 songs $7.99

Irish Songs
00312078   9 songs $6.99

The Lion King
00292062   5 songs $12.99

Modern Movie Favorites
00242674   8 songs $9.99

Movie Hits
00338187   8 songs $9.99

My First Hymn Book
00311873   12 songs $9.99

Over the Rainbow and Other Great Songs
00102098   10 songs $7.99

Pirates of the Caribbean
00123473   8 songs $10.99

Pop Hits
00123295   8 songs $9.99

Pop Super Hits
00311209   8 songs $7.95

Praise & Worship
00311044   8 songs $7.95

The Sound of Music
00310249   8 songs $10.99

Star Wars
00322185   10 songs $10.99

Star Wars: A Musical Journey
00322311   15 songs $14.99

Star Wars: Selections
00321903   9 songs $10.99

Best of Taylor Swift
00234871   8 songs $10.99

Today's Hits
00277909   8 songs $8.99

The Very Best of Broadway
00311039   8 songs $7.95

HAL•LEONARD®

View songlists and order online from your favorite music retailer at **halleonard.com**

Disney characters & artwork TM & © 2021 Disney

Prices, contents and availability are subject to change without notice.

0521
358